MW01250482

DE
WARNINGS

Poems by
Fred Muratori

BASFAL Books

DESPITE REPEATED WARNINGS

Published by BASFAL Books
517 S. Main Street
Lima, Ohio 45804

Cover art:
Richard Oelze, "Expectation" [Erwartung]. 1935-36.
Oil on canvas, 32 1/8" x 39 5/8".
THE MUSEUM OF MODERN ART, NEW YORK.
Photograph © 1994 The Museum of Modern Art, New York.

Cover design by Dan Jankowski.

Library of Congress Cataloging-in-Publication Data

Muratori, Fred, 1951—
    Despite repeated warnings: poems/by Fred
Muratori
        p.   cm.
ISBN 0-7880-0143-4
I. Title.
PS3563.U7225D47   1994
811'.54—dc20   94-7993
                                              CIP

Acknowledgments

Some poems in this volume—many in differing versions—initially appeared in the magazines credited below.

Alembic, "Eurydice on the Road"; *Blue Buildings*, "Christ Brings Light to the Provinces"; *Caesura*, "Nocturne"; *Chariton Review*, "The Screen"; *Chowder Review*, "Variation on a Koan"; *Colorado-North Review*, "The Stoic Tries to Help"; *Creeping Bent*, "The Fiction Maker," "Vestige"; *Embers*, "The Re-emergence of the Trombone"; *The Formalist*, "Philip Larkin Meets Gertrude Stein"; *La Fusta*, "Dreaming of Connecticut," "The Psychiatrist to His Favorite Patient," "Departing Sons"; *The Hollins Critic*, "The Real Muse"; *Kansas Quarterly*, "Vita Poetica"; *Lowlands Review*, "Writing Home"; *Montana Review*, "Life of an Unknown Painter"; *New England Review*, "The Guardian Angels' Recall"; *Outerbridge*, "After Meredith," "On Ruining Beethoven's Fifth Piano Concerto"; *Poetry Northwest*, "Confessional Poem," "The Relatives Will Not Be Stopped"; *Quarterly West*, "Twenty Miles from Ground Zero"; *South Coast Poetry Journal*, "A Dream of Light"; *South Dakota Review*, "Almost an Elegy"; *The Spectator* (UK), "Despite Repeated Warnings," "The Possible"; *Syracuse Poems*, "Retention & Dissipation"; *Syracuse Scholar*, "The Link"; *Tendril*, "The Casket Maker's Proposal"; *Zone 3*, "Plant Closing."

A number of poems also appeared in a limited-edition chapbook, *The Possible*, published by State Street Press. Several poems were reprinted in volumes of the *Anthology of Magazine Verse.* "The Re-emergence of the Trombone" was reprinted in *Mixed Voices* (Milkweed Editions, 1991).

CONTENTS

I. Omens

II. Last Chances

III. Hindsight

To my father, and in memory of my mother.

I. OMENS

THE RE-EMERGENCE OF THE TROMBONE

In the 19th century concert hall
with its hardbacked wooden seats,

its wooden walls and hanging lamps,
there is a silence made from trees,

a silence that roots. The violins
now resting on their players' laps

are wooden, too, and the piano
is a felled trunk given angles.

No wonder Cubists loved the musical.
No wonder Cubist paintings looked

like stained glass, which exists
here also, surrounded by mahogany.

Daylight filters through the panes
as if through summer leaves, dappling

the conductor's folded hands with green.
It is so quiet, the mind imagines

a ticking clock, wooden, with a pendulum.
One by one, the members of the audience

wake up, nudge each other,
brush sawdust from their eyes.

At the darkest corner of the stage
they spot a small but brilliant glint

of brass, growing larger, getting
brighter as it rises to its voice.

DEPARTING SONS

They linger at the station
with their thoughts and heavy packs,
cold coming in,
a continent of clouds.

The train, too, steams in slowly.
It accomplishes their parting,
the steps they haven't heart
to take themselves.

When its whistle shakes the spice jars
on the sill, the storm panes
barely set for winter,
fathers stop their raking.
A few leaves sift away, get caught
in hedges, fly again.

The sun that lures their sons
from home slips gracefully below
the life that's lived in sleep,
and geese passing south abandon
shadows on the parents' roofs.
A next day must begin, or forever hold
them in this place: the cold backwater
their steep love makes.

THE LINK

There were days dark
pterodactyls rose

like capes above the tree line,
wingspans vast, improbable.

By a brook I followed footprints
big as flagstones, almost round,

that disappeared in water
and never emerged on the opposite bank.

Heavy rain turned the woods to jungle,
an aggressive menagerie

of dragonflies, of black trunks
writhing like huge saurians.

I could blink into a world
that had no place for small boys.

I'd be the frail white thing
that couldn't camouflage itself,

there being no precedent for it,
just me, dwarfed in humid air

by languid vines and leaves
the size of suit coats.

I'd tell myself exactly who I was
and not believe it, forget parents

forget school, the missing tonsils,
forget that time crawled all around me,

paws still part fin.
I could forget a time was coming

when woods would just be woods, trees
trees, and the closest link between me

and this excavation of a memory not mine
would be the garden snake I'd jab

with a spade, sweating hard,
chopping till my heart slowed down.

THE REAL MUSE

He hovers at the back door,
biting his cigar, always buttoning,
unbuttoning, his raincoat.

He is nondescript, no long scars,
no fierce recession of the hairline.
When I approach him he acts

as if he owns the place: an impatience
with the lawn, that nailed-down look.
I've met his kind before.

The phone calls that precede them
are hysterical, cluttered with loud radios
and voices gathering coherence,

then the dial tone, then the quiet.
They never mean me any good.
But now one waits for me again,

shadows darkening above his upper lip
as if the things he's about to say
were burning their way through.

This time the stories have beginnings
and smell of incense, at times of brandy.
As I fall into his tales' reach

he frisks me for an inner life,
leaves me wordless, mistaken,
one doorway from the perfect ending.

LIFE OF AN UNKNOWN PAINTER

Standing at his closet,
he stares at velvet sleeves
and woolen shoulders, and while
the weather finally
does not affect his choice
of shirt or scarf, he asks
Is the rain an olive green?
Are the buildings blackening
like sodden trees?
At which his mistress, already done
with breakfast and the classifieds,
shags the painter from the house,
begins her sure routines.

Safe in his loft, the painter
sits imagining automatons and apes
scuttling on the rooftop tiles.
He reads Poe and Hoffmann,
and when the sun permits
bright portraits by a grove
or sequined harbor, he imagines
lightning sizzles down
to sear his model's scalp.

But in the smear of night,
after mediocre love with a woman
no successful work could ever pale,
the painter slips into himself,
into a sleep as pure as death,
effaced of line and chiaroscuro,
the canvas that admits the world
his eyes refuse to bear.

DREAMING OF CONNECTICUT

Even forests small as parking lots
are fidgety with game:
quail, pheasant,
the snide, reductive fox.
I could park anywhere. Instead
I stop my car beside a fractured elm.

As is typical of dreams, the street signs
have been switched. They're written
in an alphabet of pumps and axes.
Just the same, this is home
as a liar might remember it.
I pass the pup tent I was crushed in
when the dying apple tree gave up
its heaviest limb,
and there, next to the house
some friends burned down for fun,
stands the doctor who delivered me,
the little girl he holds at gunpoint
cracking cough drops with her teeth.

Own up, Connecticut.
You were never like that.
You were the birch I stripped of bark,
thinking *Dead Sea Scrolls, papyrus*

of the the patriarchs. You were
oak leaves in my shoes, mountain laurel,
hunks of hematite
discovered like doubloons, other kids
with names as long as mine.
Without you, I'd have never known
of Yankees, Charter Oak, what it means
to live so close to Yale and not get in.

I wake up in a room where a radiator
hisses me like Hamlet his mimes.
A change of clothes, a doughnut,
and I'm waiting in the snow for a bus,
its back end trailing gasoline
as an insect trails blood. The driver,
typical as suicide, is tied to the wheel
and headed for the life
I learn reluctantly to trust.

DESPITE REPEATED WARNINGS

Catalpa trees converse in summer wind.
Imagine that they whisper *hurricane*
as leaves display their sequin sides and spin
wildly around, portending violent rain.
Our oldest instincts help enforce their hint:
the street is vacant as a lunar plain.
(Existence would rest lightly on the mind
if every omen were as well-defined.)

No slouch myself, I also run inside
and watch a film about an alien spore
that duplicates the human race, hiding
in basements, slowly taking human form
while people sleep (a kind of homicide
that kills the soul), becoming you before
you are yourself. Mother is not mother.
Each loved one is an odd, familiar other.

The breaking clouds pour out a hard white noise.
Above them, geosynchronous with earth,
a necklace of steel satellites hangs poised
in space. The images they send are worth
a thousand inner jolts: small Moslem boys
caressing automatic rifles, birth

defects near toxic sites — a longer list
would only overstate my gist,

and what good would more overstatement do?
We've seen our share of wailing women comb
through rubble for their sons, more than a few
recorded tests of the latest doomsday bomb.
If I'm no longer me, and you're not you,
what can these signals mean to us, hearts numb
from life lived second-hand, the dreams we keep
as lovers growing monstrous as we sleep.

ON RUINING BEETHOVEN'S
FIFTH PIANO CONCERTO

Someone coughs — a quickly-punctured tire
of a cough — smack dab at the moment
when the second movement of the Emperor
totters at its steepest brink of silence.

Trances fall, and the audience —
which had been bending toward that edge
as if following a spell commanding it
to peer and be drawn in — flops back.

So small a thing to ruin so large a joy.
Our bodies, released, vent their stream
of petty needs: a cigarette, a handkerchief,
a covert scratch behind the knee.

How frantically the music tries to capture us
again. It tells us we are powerful, in love,
tall as redwoods, sensate to every form
of passion, irreplaceable as Mars —

while underneath our seats creak with the weight
we tried to lose, and April raindrops hammer
on the darkened, stained-glass windows.
Exhaust fans slowly rev, as if to lift us up.

PARTICULARS

For me, the birds and trees and varied shrubberies
 go nameless, fly or sprout in anonymity,
add their hatching to the huge, accretive
 illustration we interpret as the world.
Out of kindness, friends supply detail: the brazen
 hawk that roosts within a campus cupola
is sharp-shinned, *accipiter velox;* it feeds
 on rodents, chickadees, unlucky wrens.
All I know is that it landed gracefully
 two yards away as I was walking to my car,
glanced around the darkened quad and rose again,
 unthreatening, unthreatened, a figment.

Bird watchers rise to glimpse the spotted whatsisname
 at dawn, knee-deep in a frigid marsh,
camouflaged in paramilitary gear from L.L. Bean.
 Hush! The morning call. The telltale bobbing twig.
Suddenly a whoosh and flap, the dart of binoculars—
 while I'm at home in bed, still dreaming
of a faceless woman whose name is almost at my tongue,
 whose tongue is almost at my mouth, whose kiss
is like the misty sun just breaking from the hills....
 Gone. Frightened by a deejay weatherman,
his voice a blare of bright prediction:
 What dazzling light! Unrelenting definition!

27

Is that an aspidistra? Could the speckled alder cast
        its shadow this far south? In winter, can you tell
the autumn willow from *salix gracilis*? Each object
        extends a history entwined with legends,
with other objects and their legends, and all these
        knitted histories solidify below us, cushioning
our footsteps, preventing us from plummeting
        too deeply toward ourselves, toward that place
of infinite, receding blankness. But the ground mole
        hurries for its grub, the white squirrel
for its buried nut, as vines discreetly weave
        the death-masks of their hosts. I toss and heave

and walk the aimless, after dinner miles seeing
        nothing but paving stones, a few dead leaves
whose shapelessness I must transmute to wings
        or palms or jagged hearts that cut against
our lifelines, bit by bit and year by year.
        For some there is unending delectation
of the intricate known by its proper names,
        its habitats and rarities. For others — people
less adept at telling cirrus clouds from altostratus—
        the blurry whole, its parts compacted, dense,
an undistinguished night pressed heavily
        and without passion on the sleeper's lips.

WRITING HOME

Yet another moon poem.
But face it, if not
for her, we'd hardly ever
come home not ourselves,
picking scarabs from thin hair
or hungry for stuffed peppers.
Instead we'd stay up thinking
how we should've bought saran wrap
when it was on sale, or how
the Honda needs a tune-up, or
what fools we were for rushing
into marriage.
What's worse, we'd act as if
our living rooms were real,
as if the destinies of genes
were set efficiently inside us,
immovable as heirloom dinnerware.
But with the moon above us
like a perfect test score, we
sense the insufficiency
of common goals, the public good,
and though we ceaselessly invite
the obvious, only quirky details
crash our thoughts. We wonder
why our lymph nodes are so diligent

and why, when everybody else writes home
to say the evening is lovely
and lonesome as the moon it gives away,
we feel like running miles,
skimming our pointed shadows
across the whitened fields.

II. LAST CHANCES

PLANT CLOSING

Forget the redevelopment.
There's no incentive now.
The shops are dark by five.
The night shift's been sent home.

Take a walk along the park
at sunset, past moldering memorials
and shredding flags, and watch
the neighbors watching you

from sinking porches.
Grayer now, their hands too little used,
they were bred to breed
the unremarkable: the gears

and cogs, the metal frames,
armatures, gaskets —
inner things, undetectable
as atoms in a human eye.

If they have other lives in mind
the mind is where they live,
in celestial offices,
on aqueous putting greens.

No time, they'll sigh at daybreak,
rising as though a whistle
might still summon them
to make a part the whole is missing.

THE GUARDIAN ANGELS' RECALL

Halos blocked, satchels crammed
with silk robes like parachutes:
the Sunday best of those for whom
eternity is Sunday.
The children miss them most, left
to challenge traffic on their own.
How they cried when the horizon
grew gauzy with a billion wings,
their guardians ascending like chimney smoke.
And we adults, who knew our mortal blessings
could be no more than compliments,
wished to cry ourselves.
Driving now, we are cautious to extremes,
but the Catholic schools we pass,
their flags at half-mast, remind us
mile after mile that the strength
to save our lives has not diminished,
nor has the earth grown darker.
We must speak loudly.
We must recreate the certainties
and hide no nightmare.
As the world rebalances beneath us,
we'll hold our place.

CHRIST BRINGS LIGHT TO THE PROVINCES

Light was all the rage that year
and when he claimed it
the populace fell round itself
concentrically in swoons
and offered him their loyalty,
their sons, their feisty goats.
Tired of stubbing their toes,
of groping for doorknobs in the dark,
they called on him to end them,
imagining the afterlife as advertised.

He only stood there, fragile
as a seahorse tooth, holding
their dogged love like a bag
filled with broken glass.
Then he walked right past them
till he came to the forest
of a nation without eyes or windows.
There, rising up on just one inhalation,
he smiled down benignly on the trees,
then burst the air sharply
like a ruptured hive of livid bees,
shedding ashes and scales
in a blizzard of redress.

NOCTURNE

Curled spine to spine, like fetal twins already turned
apart, our single shape must, from above,
resemble a large Rorschach blot.
Look, an aerial observer might
cry, *a severed swan felled squarely, if not*
bloodlessly, in halves. I'm awake, and half in love.

Because she carelessly forgot to pull the drapes
completely closed, I woke to the moon's light.
Dazed, I watched it glaring overhead
as patients watch a surgeon's lamp
before the anesthetic hits, or the white-
masked, sterile face that says *Relax. Pretend you're dead.*

It draws me to the window, promising itself,
all brilliance and autonomy. I'm not swayed.
My gaze slips downward to the street
where jagged bats cavort beneath
a lamppost, cutting through a snowy spray
of gypsy moths as it spirals upward toward the bulb.

She snores, distanced safely from my thoughts. Wrapped
       skin-tight
in her sleep, she walks across the Seine or

rides canal boats across Amsterdam.
Who could compete against that store
of quiet claims: *Here it's different, here
your life will float as if on water.* Is it right

that we should hold each other back from what we want?
I'll wish she'd seen this night, how everything
within it whirlpools: bats, moths, stars
stirred to movement by the rounding
of the earth, which turns wholly for our sake,
or so they tell us. I'm in love, and half awake.

IN THE COCOON

Busy with technique,
I hadn't noticed how
the light had gone,

only that my work
had quieted. My work,
which is my mind

dragged slowly through
a field of comprehensions,
dawdling frequently

to look at dragonflies
or paw prints in the soft
and warming soil,

forgetting in the scent
of leaves and weed stalks
just what it's doing there,

but realizing vaguely
that a stress or a rhyme
is called for. Called for

by whom? Oh yes, the one
who squints at paper
in the dusk, his stomach

grumbling, his tongue
at war with words, never
satisfied, never satisfied.

AFTER MEREDITH

What are we first?
– George Meredith
Modern Love

What are we last? Last, names penned in Bibles,
anecdotes at Christmas time. Before that, clothes
in cartons destined for the drop-off box,
bills left unpaid, sealed letters in the trash,
the sides of contracts dropped before fulfillment
like bureaus from the movers' hands. Prior still,
a creaking divan on a porch, a half-drained
glass of milk, the afterthought friends think
recovering in cold, white rooms, rainwater
on the sill below a window left ajar.
Last, we are the shards of life, and life is far
beyond remeasurement. Who can, with certainty,
reconstruct a planet from a rock,
shape a body from a fingerprint?
A hand that once enclosed another left its glove
for us, there, palm up in the brown, departing leaves.

TWENTY MILES FROM GROUND ZERO

Sigmund tried to tell us: that it was nothing
we could vanquish through love or good intentions.
That it was in us sure as heart, inflexible as bone.

Though we've gathered every candle we could find
and set them burning on the cellar floor,
the darkness won't leave us alone.

It crouches by the furnace, leaps out.
We feel the continent grind upward,
our complicated century uprooted and on its way

to glowing, comprehensible fragments.
We can say now what we've truly thought.
But above the sizzling wind, the sound

of lurching stone and timber, we hear only our own
heartbeats, like footsteps coming nearer
as the minutes slow, patient and unstoppable.

THE PSYCHIATRIST TO HIS FAVORITE PATIENT

Once you receive the heavy gloves,
the coat that whispers like a serpent
when you slide your arms along
its inner skin, there is no cause
I can make for you. I just wave
and pack the snow to slippery glass.

When the window skates down sharply
on your hand, breaking no bones
but reminding you that openness
is transient, a placebo for the guilty
then you'll know the world can't
love you always, or keep your diaries
secret anymore. I'll help you find a road
that follows as it leads.

I know the pet names of the pharaohs,
and I know the names you call
your separate fingers, their quiet journeys,
their returns. It's my job
to say you're doing fine, keep trying.
It's my feral pride, my prize deception.
When you listen and take heart, I'll cast
my bones in random clutters with your own,
I'll lose myself to you whenever you are lost.

THE RELATIVES WILL NOT BE STOPPED

Uncanny, how they picked the one bad day
in twenty, the worst Sunday in a season
remembered for its photo-via-satellite:
a tide of clouds that blanked a hemisphere.

You were barely up for breakfast when
they started out, packing their Oldsmobile
full with red-faced, whining children,
their driveway littered with crushed toys.

And while that steel monster dragged its
clattering tailpipe through marshy streets,
you were groping for the coffee, trying
to find the only cup you wouldn't need

to rinse, thinking of how terrific Jane or Greta
(which was her real name?) looked while
she was sleeping, so good you lost your yen
for caffeine and crept back to the bedroom.

And the rain had already lasted centuries,
and the water in the basement lifted tupperware
and canned goods like small boats in a harbor,
and you and Greta were the only humans left

after a great flood had washed the paper boys
and Jehovah's witnesses from the sidewalks,
after a deluge had carried off
the missiles and atomic submarines. Just lips

on skin, rain sheeting down the window pane
like a constant plunge of guillotines, and Greta
(yes! it's Greta!) taking charge this time,
and you in bare amazement thanking God for His

timely retribution, unable to imagine
any other moment in your life to match this.
But some silent nerve, some quisling cell within
you must have known, must have sensed Behemoth

on its balding, slightly under-inflated tires
parting the seas to your house, its belly crammed
with undigested brats all screaming for release,
for compassion, for a tissue, for a Coke.

In your reverie and sudden shock of love
you couldn't know. The drowned world floated by
and cries for help were yelps of pleasure
melting into raindrops on your staunch roof.

Yet only blocks away a vinyl-topped sedan from hell
made the last right turn to your place, its course
sure despite the bickering its occupants spat out.
You and Greta stretched the very fabric of your

souls, reinventing gravity, geometry, gymnastics.
And as if it were an archetypal pattern, a vestige
of the species' first crude thought, you played
the Mountie and the Maiden. The room swirled

while just beyond your lawn the huge beast halted
and threw its insides out: cousins, nephews,
flabby aunts you hardly knew, still dressed up
from church, still squawking in the downpour.

How could you know they had but one terrifying wish:
to enter through the front door, track mud across
the oriental rug, and devour your homemade muffins.
How could you, when, at that moment, on a frozen peak,

you discovered Greta silhouetted like a goddess
with Aurora Borealis shyly flickering behind her?
How could you hear them calling after years
across the wastes of northern Canada had led you here?

THE WRONG TRAIN

From the window of a railway car
between Den Haag and Amsterdam
the train seems to move backward
and, at times, to stand still,
the landscape sliding past:

high-rise monoliths on treeless flats,
then red and yellow swaths of tulip fields
endowed with motion, mission,
earth fanning toward its edge.
I try to focus on a single flower,

to see the character composed by petals
on a single stem, to pinpoint one
May Wonder, and to follow it until
each of us has lost the other. But no,
our worlds are contradictory and quick.

The travelers heaped around me seem asleep.
Their gazes angle down to the floor,
their profiles darkly sloped against
the outer blue-green blur. A man's face
twitches like a sleeping watchdog's ear.

Suddenly another train blares by us,
rolling in the opposite direction,
its passengers talking, smiling, touching
glasses — daubs of color in the window panes.
A woman flashes into beauty, disappears.

I picture them arriving, embracing lovers
on a station platform marked HOME,
hands under each other's clothes
tentative with wonder and relief.
I can smell their fragrant wines,

the steaming shellfish laid out neatly
on white tablecloths, nearly feel
the cool air glancing off their backs
as they make love in waves
of Battersea and Aureola.

Their almost-lives awaken me,
and my other mind — the one that thrives
on intuitions of disaster,
suggestions of mad killers in the woods —
cries *Stop slow down slow down*

as if it could be heard above the rails.
The conductor turns, unsmiling, palm out
for the ticket crumpled in my hand
like a number in a lottery
long decided, irrevocably won.

VARIATION ON A KOAN

If a tree falls in the forest,
a large tree,
one of those redwoods
cars can drive through,

falls just suddenly,
without fanfare of high wind
or earthquake,
but smoothly, as in a scythe's arc,

and if it seems to pause
an instant from its sure-to-be
colossal impact, like something
conscious of effects,

seems to pause with the grace
of a woman briefly questioning
her heart's won wisdom,
who just as gracefully

shrugs the notion off,
seems in fact to live and die
while you and I watch the miracle
as if one of us created it,

then would we hear the sound
beneath the sound of our imagining?

A DREAM OF LIGHT

Sudden as a thunderclap, a beatific whiteness cleaves
the winter midnight, and wakes me just in time
to sense my childhood bedroom rising solidly around me,
its rafters hewn from memory, its hardwood floor intact.

Even the window is authentic, and when I draw the curtain
back, what should I see but neighbors, or the ghosts
of neighbors, running from their yards and driveways
toward the street. And following their upraised arms,

craning till my cheek adheres, frozen, to the pane,
I find the moon has swelled to several times its size,
settled high above the trees whose shadows fan
like fractures over shimmering white lawns.

The neighbors merge into a choir of amazement, resembling
in their robes and nightgowns nothing if not angels.
But one stands farther off, hesitant, not quite
persuaded, his human breath betrayed by vapor

in the unenlivened air. Sensing my gaze, he turns—
my father — his face a blurry disc of silver swerving
from the rest, and as he turns the brilliant beam
his face reflects breaks gently on my face.

I step back nearly blinded, breathing in the light.

THE POSSIBLE

The crickets in their meadows call for mates.
A high, insistent bowing scores the air,
and, like the keenest scores, it orchestrates
a mood. The moonless night displays a rare
and varied brilliance, stars so plentiful
they imitate the lights of some great city
viewed from fifteen thousand feet, attainable
though distant, a plain of possibility
which the pilot, in his kindness, tips
a wing to let us see, affording just
a glimpse of what's below before it slips
forever from our sight. We learn to trust
such moments, and derive from them a taste
of what we are, or what we are to face.

CAPTURES

Finally the evening
catches up with me.
I was smug at noon,
thinking I had lost
its scout, my shadow,
through the morning's
plot of feints
and subtle dodges.
It crept back at one.
It was only having lunch.
By five it slipped ahead
of me, taunting,
and my eyes became
mistrustful as it pooled
in rifts and hollows.
Now the sun is falling
quite perceptibly
and the sky is scarred
with livid contrails.
The hills have lost
themselves within
a single spine, black
against the limit
of this world.
Caught again, as I

always will be,
I fail to discern
my hands and heartbeat
from the night. I only
live one life
but each day something
in it happens,
unrecollectable,
that almost makes me think
I almost got away.

III. HINDSIGHT

PROGRESS

Each morning at the window
regardless of the snow
or green glow on the sill,
I hope to see it, though

I don't know what it looks like.
Should there be wind?
Should geese precede it
in a fragile, penciled wedge?

It seems to be the point
of why we're here, why we live
in fear of backwardness,
of paved streets breaking down

to shattered rock and dust,
in fear of slow forgetting,
mistrusting anything too simple.
But each morning at the window,

regardless of the variance
in temperature and light,
the world stays where it was
when we had left it for our dreams.

Only when we turn, sighing,
to our lives, do we notice
how the furniture has moved
or darkened where we've touched it.

THE CASKET MAKER'S PROPOSAL

Ten years out of high school, long enough to know
that summer's nothing special after all, I was hauling
boxes out of state, a major sale for a little man like me.

She asked to come along, needed a rolled-down window
and that sense of stillness you get from moving fast.
I said sure because I never took her out enough.

We drank beer till our tongues fell free as loose change
jangling on the sidewalk. And then, deaf from road noise,
caskets on the flatbed fit to rock right through the cab,

I popped it. Just asked like it was *What time is it?*
and blind with love's sudden puff, she kissed me going 70.
All I could think about was owls when you find one

out of happenstance, and you'd believe the whole white moon
was taking off not three yards from your face.
She was thinking, *Finally, finally. He's not much*

but at least his work is steady as it comes.
We passed a three-car pile up in the eastbound lane,
big toys some giant kid tossed topsy-turvy.

Like anybody else we gawked. It was the first time
I'd ever seen a dead man out of formal clothes,
splayed over a guardrail, his head dangling in the weeds.

I thought, *Death is real. But so is everything this woman
sitting next to me will do or say to make it less so.*
I turned on the radio to find the song we'd need to remember.

EURYDICE ON THE ROAD

The valley's lights dissolve
     into the trees.
     We drive uphill
and blood washes backward
to our spines, soothing
as an evening bath.

This is not our first attempt.
     There were times when
     each school recess
sent us running for high fences,
     times our parents
dragged us back from town lines
as we cried to trains that slipped
like earthworms into red horizons.

Now we'll be erasures
     on the census,
     given up, despised.
The road jars us with ruts.
The wine we share is warm, not far
from vinegar and nearly gone.
     This escape is not
     what I imagined

and something in me wants to say
Turn back, one town is like another.

But your eyes are like a wolf's.
     The radio plays
      songs we used to
dance to in the gym. You never
even glance up to the rearview.
     I turn and see
the roadsides flashing red
      then white then red,
hear sirens calling in the voices
we've obeyed most of our lives.

You drop from second gear
      to first , teeth clenched,
      grunting *bastards*
as we slow. This meant a world
to you. My door opens so easily
I know that it was never closed.

RETENTION & DISSIPATION

When the lines of her body slide
in elegant silhouette against the sun-fused shade
of my bedroom window,
and when the line of her mouth spreads
into a faintly taunting arc,
I think, *Ingres you were right.*
   The line is all.
   It is the endless vein
that holds the energy of being in continual flow.

But when the cold pulls color to her face
like October wind coaxing Autumn's blood
to the skin of a leaf,
I think, *Delacroix, how could anyone doubt*
   that color draws all things together
   like a glue that binds and permeates,
the very shadow of our souls, seeping into life.

And when her smile reflects tired suns and
fluorescent lights, full moons and marquees,
I see the things that shrink the pupils
of childrens' eyes.
   Like Vermeer's glowing maid, she gives
my barren kitchen a proud depth,
an undeserved gravity.

But as she falls away from me
toward a lover who paints her future on a larger canvas,
I say, *Man, you were an idiot.*
  Only speech controls. It suspends
  the smallest motion, shatters any fear
or dark speculation in the space of a word.

  Her image fades from my mind's gallery
like a figure from Leonardo's supper,
arms half-raised in wonder or abandonment.
  Swallowing seems difficult
and I remember that my mouth
was once deep-chambered, and hot.

THE SCREEN

We watch films of actors suffering
from love or axe wounds.
Pain's causes fail to matter
since we marvel only at the swoons,
mad scenes, the bitter partings
into which we substitute ourselves.
Our lips move in the dark.

We choose the sides of those most wronged
and least able to get even.
Crushing the soft drinks in our hands
we yearn to get even. Even.
For a time the actors bear the worst
with dignity and promise,
fine taste in clothes intact.

When they can hold it in no longer
they maim themselves, or strangers.
We understand why. Our palms crease
in the same inevitable places.
The actors love the way we'd like to—
in furious waves, breath steaming off
the places kissed, bodies redefined in fire.

Whether things end well or grimly,
concrete life waits for us outside
like a patient spouse.
We are late getting back to it.
The slow walk up the aisle carpet
creates a static in our souls.
We come out charged. We have escaped.
But those we love insist we never change.

PHILIP LARKIN MEETS GERTRUDE STEIN

I wonder what it is that so allures us,
Why we sail, or fly, or walk so readily
To Twenty-seven rue de Fleurus.

Grim Miss Toklas keeps one entertained
With *eau-de-vie*, but in a joyless way,
And in honesty I'd say the time is strained

Until Miss Stein herself appears, not quite
Magnificent, not quite as one's imagined.
She says she's read my poetry in spite

Of what *the others* say. Who these others
Are I couldn't guess, and even if I knew,
No loss of sleep. Poets aren't brothers

After all. I don't know what I'm doing here,
And why, with Spring about to lighten Hull,
I let this gabbing woman bend my ear.

No, I've never relished *Finnegans Wake*.
Tom Hardy's more my style, Marvell, Donne.
This modern racket only glorifies what's fake.

Oh dear, it seems I've crossed a boundary line.
It's *Adieu, Mr. Larkin, come again.*
I shiver slightly, and decline.

CONFESSIONAL POEM

The moon is sludge gray, pin-striped
in places like a patchwork suit.
My blood is the color of Colby cheese
and each night, after dinner gets cold,
I open my wrist with a potato peeler.

Never in my life have I practiced
before mirrors.
Both parents loved me dearly.
I got A's in school.
My car gets fantastic gas mileage.
There's nothing in my dresser drawers
anyone would be afraid to touch.

I tell you these things
because I long for your resentment.
I want you to skirt me widely
and pretend that I don't matter.
I want you to look away.
What I do is better left to shadow
and to gray-green landscapes
that would not support the barest life.

THE FICTION MAKER

His story wanted altitude,
a place to find its wings.
He gave it time and trial,
and when late Fall apples
rotted brown on bare branches
he let the story loose.

Dogs joined its romp, and quail
blustered from the weeds
before them. Clouds spun
and balanced on the treetops
like dishes on a juggler's pole.

He kept his porch light burning
for it, and through the winter
he could hear it brush the house,
whistling tunes around
the silent center he'd become.

Snowbanks rose higher
than his living room windows
as if to seal him from the world,
but he was learning to be happy
from books that promised happiness.

Finally a slow thaw lured him out
among the new, emboldened buds.
He saw his story floundering
atop an oak, caught in branches
smaller than his fingertips.

Its future seemed unsolvable, but
it wasn't his problem anymore,
nor his passion, nor his love.
He watched it struggle in the wind,
a gust away from heaven,
pretending it had never known him.

VITA POETICA

There are words I need.
They are not near men.
— Charles Simic

Always just you and me, long after
everyone has eaten, after children hear
the whispered *ever afters* in their sleep
and lovers part to let their bodies dry
against designer-patterned sheets.

Just you and me, alone, awake
to meter out the lineation of our life
together, the slack and stress of it,
peripheries I barely sense
while you describe, or circumscribe.

There were — are — other men and women,
and other pacts made out of earshot
no less intimate or impossible, no more
desperate than ours, no more removed
from human pulse and commerce.

Sometimes I can't remember what I am.
The night unfolds me like an unsigned
letter, lets me fall into a world worn
metal-slick and featureless by wind
and constant silence. I need you then

as I would have needed graceful arms
around my waist, a sleepy, reassuring kiss
below my ear, had things been different.
Defined in context by a touch, that life
would also be articulate, but wrong.

VESTIGE

October flare of staghorn on the roadside
guides me home, red so vibrant that at times
a pinkish shadow glimmers on the asphalt.

My imagination. But October
is the earth's imagination, allowed
one wild shedding in the moment before sleep.

The bed I'll sleep in when the road uncoils
its last familiar curve was itself
collector of a dream's fine down. How sharp

my disappointment when I'd wake with empty
hands, groping through the blanket for a child's
dreamt-up prize. Once I dreamed tornados gouged

the back yard. The sky washed red and purple,
trees wrenched free of roots, but our house stood
firm.
When the weather cleared I found a fissure

through our scrawny patch of evergreens,
and inside, fossil bones: femurs, ribs, skulls.
I scooped out a tooth before the morning came,

and, awakened, found a tooth lay in my palm —
the rootless one I'd placed beneath my pillow
believing it would be replaced with coins.

I'm driving home before the western storms
can beat me there. I come unshaven,
childless, alone, as if something waited

where I'd lost it years ago, nearly
buried in the yellow leaves, weathered smooth
but visible in quickly-failing light.

THE STOIC TRIES TO HELP

I've eaten year-old steaks and lived,
        forced myself to think
of nothing but infinity
        yet kept my brains intact.

And though I've lost a score of loves
        so deep they twined around
my bones like copper veins, I learned
        again to relish sleep

and the American short story.
        Don't ask me how I do it.
There are no charms or aerosols
        that I can recommend.

Next time you chase a midnight bus
        or a woman who's fled,
sobbing, from a restaurant you
        picked, just look for someone
snickering nearby, his fingers
        burning from the cigarette
        he thinks he's tossed away.

ALMOST AN ELEGY

The crowd gathers on the lawn
at noon, familiar melange
of Avon ladies, milkmen,
the neighbors' squirming broods.
They wait for news of your absence,
that you will soon fill a vacancy
held in your name since birth.

You breathe a textbook breath,
straighten your flannel robe,
and emerge the humble ascetic,
resplendently dull, a silhouette
against the aluminum siding's glare.
Applause is weak and sporadic.
You should have waited longer.

Friends, you say, *acquaintances,*
and those to whom I barely nod,
you come here today, attentive
and, I must say, well-behaved,
to celebrate my assumption.
But they are watching blue jays
or chewing on dandelion stems.
You decide to chuck the speech.

Stepping over tanned legs,
over dogs and fumbled ice cream,
you realize that things
will stay the same without you.
No one yells goodbye,
but half a block away you hear crying.
Or laughing. The two sound so alike
you could have filled your lifetime
telling them apart.